IMAGES
of America

WEYMOUTH

TOWN HALL CORNERSTONE. On Memorial Day 1928, more than 500 people gathered to witness the laying of the cornerstone for the new town hall. Twenty of Weymouth's 22 surviving Civil War veterans participated. Weymouth was founded in 1622 and incorporated in 1635. The completed town hall appears on page 66.

IMAGES
of America

WEYMOUTH

Debbie Sargent Sullivan and Joanne Palmieri Tighe

ARCADIA
PUBLISHING

Copyright © 2001 by Debbie Sargent Sullivan and Joanne Palmieri Tighe
ISBN 978-1-5316-0570-4

Published by Arcadia Publishing
Charleston, South Carolina

Library of Congress Catalog Card Number: 2001091357

For all general information contact Arcadia Publishing at:
Telephone 843-853-2070
Fax 843-853-0044
E-mail sales@arcadiapublishing.com
For customer service and orders:
Toll-Free 1-888-313-2665

Visit us on the Internet at www.arcadiapublishing.com

On behalf of the members of the Weymouth Historical
Society, we dedicate this book to Jane Holbrook Jewell,
the last member of the Holbrook family to be born in
the Holbrook House, in recognition of her generosity
and her support of all the society's endeavors.

CONTENTS

THE HOLBROOK HOUSE. The Jason Holbrook Homestead, built *c.* 1763, was given to the Weymouth Historical Society by the town of Weymouth. In 1968, the society moved the building to 238 Park Avenue from its original location on Pleasant Street near the corner of Park Avenue. Part of the original grounds had been used as the site for South Junior High School. The new location, formerly a corner of the Weymouth Fairgrounds, was donated to the society by developer Edward Jordan. This view shows the house sometime before 1910.

INTRODUCTION

Weymouth has the distinction of being the site of the first town meeting and the second-oldest town in the Commonwealth, behind Plymouth.

The recorded history of Weymouth begins in 1622, with the arrival of a group of adventuresome young men from England who were bent on establishing a trade outpost at the location known as Wessaguscus. After a winter that found them short on supplies and unsuccessful in their business dealings, the group dispersed in the spring of 1623.

Later that year, a larger, better-prepared contingent arrived and Weymouth was permanently established. The leaders of that group also decided to leave the area, and the remaining settlers were left to devise their own form of leadership. They wanted a system that was more egalitarian than the structure they had left behind in England, and thus was born the first town meeting. By 1630, Wessaguscus had a population of nearly 300 and was recognized as part of the Massachusetts Bay Colony.

Weymouth had sent men to participate in the Pequot War of 1637 but, in 1675, King Philip's War actually reached the town. Homes were burned and residents were killed. This is the only war that has reached into Weymouth (although, of course, Weymouth citizens participated in the French and Indian War and in the many domestic and international wars since).

After two centuries as a fishing and agricultural community, Weymouth encountered the industrial revolution. New roads brought stagecoaches and horse-drawn cars. The Old Colony Railroad began serving South Weymouth in 1845 and ran trains until 1959. Trolleys were introduced in the 1890s and soon served the whole town. Until c. 1930, trolley lines ran all over Weymouth; for years people could get to any part of town for a nickel.

By 1880, the shoe industry was the single most important industry in town, with nearly 75 shoe factories employing one-third of the population. The first shoe shop opened in 1808; the last shoe factory closed in 1973. The second-largest employer was the Weymouth Iron Works, which operated from 1837 until 1890, employing nearly 300. The granite quarries employed a similar number.

The South Weymouth Naval Air Station, established in 1943, was a busy training facility for the navy that brought in much needed revenue from the families that moved to Weymouth to be near the base. For 53 years, the base was the center of existence for thousands of servicemen from all over the country.

With the phasing out of the naval air station and the waning of the shoe industry, Weymouth gradually became a bedroom community for those working in Boston and other communities in the area.

The Weymouth Historical Society was founded in 1879 to preserve the town's history, search out Weymouth's past, and share it with the community. The society has collected and preserved thousands of artifacts, photographs, and written histories. The society's main library, at the Holbrook House, includes an extensive genealogical library, original maps, manuscripts, family histories dating back to the 1600s, and comprehensive records for most of the South Shore towns. The society has published more than a dozen books, ranging from a history of the shoe industry in Weymouth to a 900-page comprehensive history of the town, produced in 1923 in honor of the town's tercentenary. The Weymouth Historical Society also operates the Weymouth Museum, which is located in the basement of the Tufts Library on Broad Street in Weymouth Landing. The museum is open on Monday evenings and features portraits of famous Weymouth residents and mementos of Weymouth places and people, including a 600-year-old dugout canoe. Readers are invited to visit the museum or to contact the Weymouth Historical Society at 781-340-1022 for further information.

One of the society's goals is to make its collection accessible for present and future generations, but many of the objects and original photographs are in delicate condition. Although this title is an appropriate way to share its resources and draw attention to its collection, regrettably photographic images were not available for many landmarks of early Weymouth history, nor was there room for all the photographs that we wished to include.

—Debbie Sargent Sullivan and Joanne Palmieri Tighe
June 2001

One

WEYMOUTH LANDING

WELCOME TO WEYMOUTH. This 1926 photograph, looking south along Commercial Street, shows Weymouth Landing. The actual town line between Braintree and Weymouth is Smelt Brook, which runs perpendicular to Commercial Street at the lowest level in Weymouth Landing. The steeple of Sacred Heart Church, which dominates the horizon in the center, is still the tallest structure in Weymouth Landing.

THE TUFTS LIBRARY. The Tufts Library was constructed at a cost of $22,000 at the corner of Washington and Commercial Streets in 1891. The land for the library had been donated by Susan Tufts, the granddaughter of Dr. Cotton Tufts, who had practiced in Weymouth. In 1966, the building was removed to widen the intersection and provide a better traffic flow. The ground floor housed stores, then a post office branch, and finally the children's library.

WASHINGTON STREET, TOWARD WEYMOUTH LANDING. On the right side of the street in this *c.* 1910 image of Washington Street are the Universalist church (which burned in 1938), Sacred Heart Church, and the Tufts Library. On the left is the stone wall that surrounded the Weston Estate; another view of the estate is shown on page 13.

WASHINGTON STREET, TOWARD SOUTH WEYMOUTH. Looking down Washington Street at the intersection of Commercial Street, this view shows the Wales Hotel on the left. It opened in 1770 as a stagecoach stop on the route from Boston to Scituate and served people disembarking ships that docked at Weymouth Landing. It was converted into the rectory for the Sacred Heart Church in 1872 and became a convent in 1913. This site, combined with the site of the Cowing House (see page 14), is now occupied by the Sacred Heart School. The large brick building on the corner is the Tufts Library, which had just been completed; beyond it is Sacred Heart Church.

Tufts Library

WASHINGTON SQUARE. In 1879, the bequest of siblings Quincy and Susan Tufts left land and funds for establishing the library that still bears their names, although it is now operated as the public library system for the town of Weymouth. The first building to house the library had opened in 1880 at the corner of Washington and Commercial Streets, offering 2,000 volumes. Within a year, it had almost as many borrowers as books. Seen here in its original location, the building was moved to Commercial Street in 1891 and served as the town library until the new library was ready in 1892 (see page 10). The building was later occupied by the *Weymouth Gazette*. An interior view of the newspaper's offices is shown on the opposite page.

THE WEYMOUTH GAZETTE. The staff of the town newspaper poses in its offices on Washington Street *c.* 1910. Shown, from left to right, are Francis Garrity, Martha Garrity, Mellie Purchase, John O'Connor, and Mark Garrity. Power for the printing presses was supplied by a water-driven motor.

WESTON PARK. Maria Weston Chapman (1806–1885), a noted abolitionist, organized the Boston Female Anti-Slavery Society in 1832, wrote several antislavery tracts, and edited William Lloyd Garrison's paper *Liberator*. She spent her later years at the Weston Estate on Washington Street, which was acquired by the town in 1929. The area is now the park behind the main building of the Tufts Library.

13

THE COWING HOUSE. In 1803, architect Charles Bulfinch designed this brick mansion on Commercial Street for shipbuilder Samuel Arnold Jr. Known for its beautiful Colonial-style doorway and windows, the home was directly across the street from the Arnold Tavern (see page 15). Sacred Heart School now stands on this site. The debris in the foreground is the remains of the Arnold Tavern, the birthplace of Samuel Arnold, which was demolished in 1927.

THE RICHARDS HOUSE. David Richards built this home at 468 Washington Street in 1817. Mrs. Henry Richards and her dog can be seen in this 1910 view. In 1979, this building was removed and replaced by a restaurant, which in turn has been replaced by a building that houses a chain pharmacy.

14

THE ARNOLD TAVERN. Built *c.* 1741 by Capt. Alexander Nash for his new bride, the tavern stood on Commercial Street near Washington Street. Originally, the roadway had been known as the Plymouth Trail, and several of the Boston Almanacs of the late 18th century referred to the tavern as the fifth tavern out of Boston on the road to Plymouth. Here, the Committee of Correspondence, including representatives from Weymouth and nine surrounding towns, met in secret to plan strategies for defense during the Siege of Boston in 1775 and stored the powder and arms used by local militia. The tavern was torn down in 1927 to make room for a business block and a theater, which were removed in 1961. Behind the house are the columns of the Worster homestead, which still stands at 84 Commercial Street.

LINCOLN SQUARE. The first trolley cars appeared in Weymouth in 1895 and ran from Weymouth Landing to Central Square in East Weymouth. The Braintree Weymouth Trolley ran from Braintree Depot to Weymouth Landing via Elm Street and up the hill to Lincoln Square (the corner of Broad and Washington Streets) and then continued along Washington Street to Hunt and Front Streets. The fare was 5¢. This photograph was taken in 1896 in front of the Baptist church and shows Fire Station No. 3 on the left. The home in which Frank Lloyd Wright lived for three years as a child (1874–1877) can be seen above the trolley on the right.

THE FIRST BAPTIST CHURCH. The church was built in 1866 on Washington Street in Lincoln Square. As a boy, architect Frank Lloyd Wright spent many Sunday mornings here pumping the church organ while his father, Rev. William C. Wright, conducted the service.

THE UNIVERSALIST CHURCH. The Universalist church, built in 1839, stood next to Sacred Heart Church on Washington Street. After it was severely damaged by fire in 1938, the Sacred Heart Church purchased the property and later used it as a parking lot.

WEYMOUTH LANDING. This *c.* 1900 aerial photograph of Weymouth Landing shows the steeple of Sacred Heart Church on the left, the Tufts School on the horizon in the center, and the steeple of the Baptist church in Lincoln Square on the horizon on the right. The large building just to the right of Sacred Heart now houses the Sinclair Dance Studio, and the large home between the Tufts School and the Baptist church is 20 Front Street.

THE CRANE STORE. In 1836, John Crane established this store at 1 Commercial Street, where he sold boots, shoes, and galoshes. By the time of this photograph (c. 1885), the store was run by other family members. It later burned, along with three neighboring businesses.

WASHINGTON SQUARE. Standing at the corner of Washington and Commercial Streets in the 1870s, looking north, this photographer saw, from left to right, the Gaston House; John Worster Groceries, Provisions, and Billiards; P. Lane Grocers; Solon Pratt Stoves and Tinware; and Lewis Rich & Company Dry and Fancy Goods Store. The steeple in the distance belongs to the Union Congregational Church in East Braintree.

19

FRONT STREET. This view of Front Street in the 1920s features the home of Everett McIntosh at 62 Front Street on the left. McIntosh was a teacher and the parks commissioner for many years. The elm trees that once lined Front Street were lost to disease.

THE WALLACE HOUSE. This home at 97–99 Front Street was owned by John E. Hunt, a boot and shoe manufacturer in the late 19th century, and had earlier housed the Old Bill Wallace Shoe Shop.

FRONT STREET. The house on the far left in this *c.* 1900 scene is 769 Front Street, the Wilson Tirrell House. Tirrell's daughter Betsy Frances Tirrell was murdered there in 1860 by George Hersey. The case was the first in which poisoning by strychnine was medically proven. The building in the center was one of the oldest shoe shops in Weymouth. Built *c.* 1808 by James Tirrell, it served the family shoe business until *c.* 1867 and was then used for a variety of purposes until destroyed by fire *c.* 1920. The home on the far right belonged to Amos Merritt, whose daughter Susan became a noted artist and lived in the home for many years. The boys are sitting on the bridge where the Mill River flows under the road.

GAS EXPLOSION. An early-morning gas explosion on April 10, 1935, demolished the First National grocery store and broke every window in Weymouth Landing. Joseph Brown, the store's manager, had been called in to assist in pumping water from the store's flooded basement and was killed instantly in the blast. Eight other men who were in the area to help fight the floodwaters were also injured. Damage was valued at a $500,000, and federal aid was offered to help the town cope with what was described as one of the most disastrous accidents ever to occur on the South Shore.

THE HOME OF COTTON TUFTS. Built by Thomas White at 246 Commercial Street in 1696, the house was purchased in 1774 by Dr. Cotton Tufts, who added on several wings. Tufts was a state senator, a delegate to the Constitutional Convention, and a cofounder of the Massachusetts Medical Society. His grandchildren Quincy and Susan Tufts were the founders of the Tufts Library. The home still stands on the Fore River.

WEYMOUTH LANDING. The landing was flooded after five inches of rain fell on March 18, 1968. Roads were closed to all but emergency vehicles.

THE UNION CONGREGATIONAL CHURCH. Originally built on Hollis Street in Boston in 1789, the church was taken apart and moved by barge to 18 Quincy Avenue, on the Weymouth-Braintree line, in 1811. As the building was being reassembled after the move, the parishioners decided to reconstruct only one of the two original bell towers. Architect Charles Bulfinch had copied them from towers designed by Sir Christopher Wren. The clock was added in 1852. In 1897, the church was ignited by a spark from a passing train and was destroyed by the ensuing fire. Fragments of the church bell, originally cast by Paul Revere, were made into miniature bells as mementos of the old church.

Two

NORTH WEYMOUTH

THE BRADLEY FERTILIZER PLANT. Founded before the Civil War by William L. Bradley, the company moved to Weymouth Neck later in the 1800s. By 1900, the factory employed more than 1,000 people and claimed to be the largest fertilizer factory in the world. In later years, it was affiliated with the American Agricultural Chemical Company and was commonly known as Agrico. Polish workers were housed on site in the rows of cottages just above the center of the photograph; many of their descendants still live in Weymouth. After the factory closed in the 1960s, high-rise condominiums were built on the site.

LOVELL'S GROVE. At an accessible and scenic point where the Fore River joins the sea, Lovell's Grove became a popular resort area frequented by day-trippers who came by steamer from Boston. During World War II, the site was a strategic placement for machine-gun crews. Another view of this site appears on page 127.

THE SEA VIEW HOTEL. The Sea View Hotel was located on the north side of Bridge Street, near King's Cove. The hotel welcomed permanent and transient guests with good room and board for a moderate price.

ROSE CLIFF COTTAGES. Many families in South Weymouth owned cottages at Wessagussett or Fort Point to take advantage of waterfront recreation opportunities. The Fort Point trolley ran down North Street to Bridge Street, left on Neck Street, and onto River Street.

FORT POINT ROAD AND GREAT HILL. The building on the left is the back of the trolley waiting station on River Street, with the Fort Point Hotel behind it. The cottages on the right, built by squatters, were taken by the town in 1960 and used for fire department training practice.

THE NORTH WEYMOUTH YACHT CLUB. When this photograph was taken in 1934, the yacht club was preparing to celebrate its 20th anniversary and had become a significant presence in North Weymouth, with 128 members and property worth $400,000.

WESSAGUSSETT BEACH. The waterfront from Lovell's Grove to Fort Point was a popular summer resort area from the late 1800s until the 1920s. Cottages, hotels, houses, and a yacht club dotted the shoreline at the foot of Great Hill.

BICKNELL SQUARE. One of the Eastern Massachusetts Street Railway trolleys that ran between Quincy Square and East Weymouth appears in this view looking down Sea Street from the corner of Bridge Street *c.* 1900. The trolleys are long gone, but the tracks remain under the street. The Universalist church is on the left, and the Bicknell and Holbrook Shoe Factory is on the right.

GREAT HILL AND WESSAGUSSETT BEACH. On June 13, 1923, crowds awaited the arrival of Supreme Court Chief Justice William Howard Taft, who had earlier been president of the United States. Taft, a descendant of Weymouth's Torrey family, came to help the town celebrate its 300th anniversary. A memorial was placed atop Great Hill to commemorate events surrounding the arrival of Miles Standish and his army of men, who came to help the colonists in 1623.

THE ABIGAIL ADAMS HOUSE. Abigail Smith Adams, wife of one U.S. president and the mother of another, was born here in 1744. Shown at its second location at 450 Bridge Street, the house was moved again, to the corner of North and Norton Streets near its original site in 1947. The child standing in the front yard is Ann Smith. The restored house is a National Historic Landmark.

BICKNELL SQUARE. Around 1930, Bicknell Square featured Hilliard's Candy and a dentist's office next door to each other (far left). The block on the right began with Hearn Drugstore, followed by the First National, DiTullio's Barbershop, Keene's Ice Cream, and Central Motor Mart. The Edison stack can be seen in the background. The traffic officer in the crossing box is Norman Butler.

THE OLD NORTH CHURCH. This church, also known as the First Church, was built in 1833. An earlier church, built at another location in 1682, had burned in April 1751. Rev. William Smith, father of Abigail Adams, wrote: "The Meeting House burned to ashes. The town's stock of three barrels of gun powder was in the loft and made a surprising noise when it blew up."

THE WORKHOUSE. Care of the poor, elderly, and orphaned was a social problem that the town had to face in the 18th and 19th centuries. Also known as the infirmary or poor farm, this institution was located on Essex Street where the Weymouth Housing Authority now stands.

J.W. Bartlett & Company. John W. Bartlett and William O. Collyer were partners in the firm of J.W. Bartlett & Company, which was located at 33 Sea Street. They sold a wide range of dry goods and other products, including clothing, carpet, furniture, shoes, medicine, tobacco, and groceries.

Collyer's Market. A lifelong resident of Weymouth, Herman Collyer, with his daughter Velma operated a market at 9 Sea Street for 61 years before selling it in 1972. As the son of William Collyer, who owned the store above, Herman continued a family tradition. He was also a World War I veteran and the town's last "call chief" for the Weymouth Fire Department.

THOMAS CORNER. At the beginning of the 20th century, the corner of Sea and North Streets was a busy place. D.A. Jones was a news dealer and confectioner at 10 Sea Street. He also maintained the waiting room for the Old Colony Street Railway. These buildings now house European Hair Design and Pizza Plus.

PILGRIM CONGREGATIONAL CHURCH. The church was organized in June 1851 by 51 members who left the First Church of Weymouth. The new society built this church on Athens Street and dedicated it on March 11, 1852.

A GROCERY STORE. In June 1895, Walter Sladen and Isaac Holden opened a grocery store at the corner of North and Church Streets, a site that had once been the Arnold Store. The upper floors housed apartments. The store also functioned as the local post office and as a waiting room for the trolley; in the lower photograph on the opposite page, this building appears on the right, alongside the trolley tracks. In later years, the building was known as the Colonial Drug Store; the location is now the site of a block of stores that includes a 7-Eleven and Domino's Pizza.

MOUNT VERNON. This replica of George Washington's home was built *c.* 1904 at the highest point of King Oak Hill in Weymouth Heights by Civil War veteran Waldo Turner. Its vistas of the surrounding countryside range from Boston's Harbor Islands to the Blue Hills in Milton.

WEYMOUTH HEIGHTS. Sladen's store stood at the corner of North and Church Streets and is seen in this view looking up King Oak Hill from the railroad depot bridge. The Eastern Massachusetts Street Railway Trolley ran through here on its way to East Weymouth.

LIFEGUARDS AT WESSAGUSSETT BEACH. One summer in the late 1960s, the lifeguards included, from left to right, the following: (front row) Irene Burrell, Peggy McMorrow, Denise Bilodeau, Mary Cole, Jodi Brattan, Ginny Dwyer, Judy Riley, Terry Bilodeau, and Judy Brattan; (middle row) Mary Hoyle, Susan Clark, Nancy Clark, unidentified, Deborah Ryan, Joanne Murphy, Diane Hoyle, Jane Richardson, Carol Geddes, and unidentified; (back row) Edmund Rainsford, Jim Ewen, Jerry McDonald, William Neiland, Brad Cleaves, unidentified, Billy Fallon, Larry Morrison, Gerry Fallon, and Ted Hoyle.

Three

SOUTH WEYMOUTH

THE FOGG OPERA HOUSE. When the Fogg Opera House opened in 1888 at the corner of Columbian and Pleasant Streets, the *Weymouth Gazette* proclaimed it to be "one of the handsomest and costliest structures in the state," describing in detail its oak paneling and marble staircases, as well as the grand hall and theater in its upper reaches. This view from 1919 shows the ground floor occupied by the post office. A bank, bowling alley, and clubroom occupied the other levels. The church on the right is the Old South Union Congregational Church; on the left is the Second Universalist Church.

VIEW IN COLUMBIAN SQUARE 1875

COLUMBIAN SQUARE 190

COLUMBIAN SQUARE. The upper photograph shows Columbian Square in 1875 with ancient elm trees and a water pump. The small square building on the left is Rogers Hall, where dances were held and where South High School held its classes until 1874. The home on the right belonged to John Reed. By 1902, the major buildings of Columbian Square were in place: the Fogg Opera House (left of center), the Old South Union Congregational Church, and the Fogg Library (far right).

COLUMBIAN SQUARE. This aerial view shows Columbian Square during the 1930s while it still had the traffic rotary, seen in the lower-right corner. Above the rotary is the Fogg Library, built in 1898 of Weymouth's own seam-faced granite. The Fogg Opera House, center, is shown in its original form, before storefronts were added. The Second Universalist Church is to the left of the Fogg Opera House, and the Old South Union Congregational Church is above and to the right.

POSTAL CARRIERS. In this 1907 photograph, the postal carriers based in the Fogg Opera House in Columbian Square pose with the first parcel post to arrive in Weymouth. The gentleman standing farthest to the right is Elbridge Nash, and Burt Lord is driving the wagon.

THE FOGG LIBRARY. John S. Fogg, a banker and boot manufacturer, bequeathed $50,000 for the construction of a building to be used as a hall for public assemblies and the storage of books. This fine example of Italian Renaissance architecture, built in 1898 of seam-faced granite with rare Brisi stained-glass windows, is included in the U.S. Park Department's National Register of Historic Places.

LOUD'S LIVERY. In the 1880s, Wilbur Loud maintained a livery stable on Union Street; this load of hay is destined for the stable. He also sold horses, fertilizer, hay, and coal. In the background, down Union Street, are the arches of the Fogg Opera House in Columbian Square.

ELBRIDGE NASH'S DRUG STORE. Nash's occupied one corner of the first floor of the Fogg Shoe Factory in Columbian Square from 1875 until the 1960s. The store offered not only drugs, medicines, and toiletries but also goods ranging from candy and tobacco to stationery and cutlery.

THE FOGG SHOE FACTORY. Built in 1857, the factory at the corner of Pleasant and Union Streets, later known as the Fogg Building, was the first of its kind in Weymouth to have an elevator. By the early 1940s, the building housed Elbridge Nash's Drug Store, Juliedde Dress Shop, Mabel Proctor Dry Goods, the South Weymouth Cooperative Bank, and Paul's Barbershop, although most of the building was occupied by M.R. Loud Hardware.

JESSEMAN'S HARDWARE. From 1843 until 1872, this building served as the Union Church. Later, a second story was added and the upper part was used as a music hall. In 1957, the building was replaced by a new store with apartments on the upper floors. The building on the left is that of McGaw's News.

COLUMBIAN SQUARE. This view of Columbian Square, looking south down Pleasant Street, shows Dondero's Store, the First National supermarket (which has been Olden's Drug Store since 1941), Jesseman's (now the site of the Chauncy Building), and the fire station. On the right is Jansen's five-and-dime store, where Fosters' Gallery is now.

PLEASANT STREET. This view, looking east from the belfry of Old South Union Church c. 1865, shows the spacious, comfortable homes of 19th-century South Weymouth. The barn in the right foreground belonged to Melvin Raymond, and the home just to the right of it to Josiah Torrey. The large white house in the center is now the C.C. Shepherd Funeral Home on Pleasant Street, and the house above and to the left of it, featuring a mansard roof and cupola,

belonged to Prince Tirrell. Across the street from Abbott was Dr. Levine, and the home farthest to the left belonged to Mrs. Marshall Abbott. In the upper-right corner of the picture, the home with a cupola and mansard roof was the Josiah Reed estate and is now Whittaker's Nursing Home on Union Street.

INDEPENDENCE SQUARE. In this view of the square, looking down Pond Street toward the railroad station, the large white house in the center stands on the corner that is now occupied by Walgreens.

WILDEY LODGE. The cornerstone of the Odd Fellows Hall in Independence Square (at the intersection of Main and Pleasant Streets) was laid with much ceremony in 1880, including a box containing various coins and documents. After several renovations that incorporated much streamlining, the building now houses a retail shop and several apartments. Its neighbors remain largely unchanged, including the Simon Joy House (on the right), which was built c. 1737 at 22 Pleasant Street.

46

EARLY-20TH-CENTURY INDEPENDENCE SQUARE. At the beginning of the 20th century, children were often taken to school in these horse-drawn carriages, which were also known as barges. This view of the square, looking south at the intersection of Pleasant, Pond, and Main Streets, is now the site of Liberty Travel (on the right) and the Marshall's Plaza (which replaced the buildings on the left). In the 18th century, this was the site of the town stocks, where offenders who had violated various town ordinances were placed, to be subjected to the jeers of small boys and other citizens.

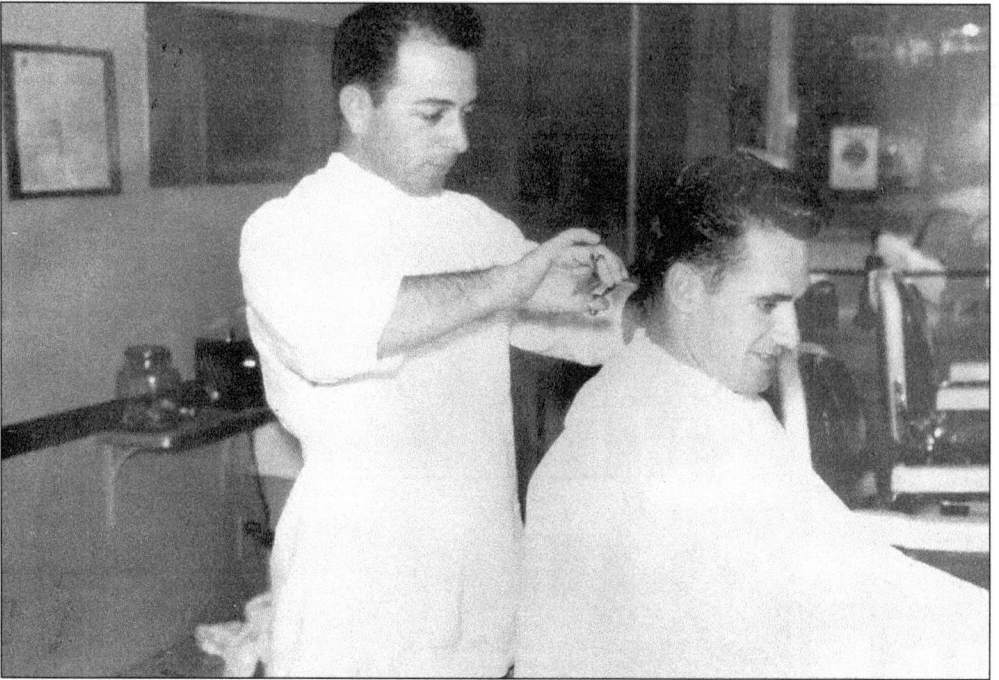

BARBERS. At Blackwell's Barbershop, *c.* 1957, Dick Ortenzi cuts Al Perette's hair. Perette still operates Al's Barbershop on Union Street, which he established in 1963. In 1973, Blackwell's burned down and Ortenzi opened Dick's Barbershop, behind Olden's Pharmacy.

THE CHARLES BROWN STORE. Brown sold meat, fish, and provisions. The post office now occupies this site on Pleasant Street in Columbian Square. Descendants of Frank Crosby (seated on the steps) still live in Weymouth.

THE OLD SOUTH UNION CHURCH. The Second Parish in Weymouth built its first meetinghouse in 1723, replaced it in 1784–1785, and, in 1853, built the present structure. In May 1989, careless use of an electric paint remover started a fire that caused more than $1 million in damage, but the church has been completely restored. The church can also be seen on pages 38 and 39.

THE BENJAMIN FRANKLIN WHITE HOUSE. This home at 937 Main Street housed the offices of the South Weymouth Savings Bank when it opened in 1868. The original bank offices were in a room to the extreme right; a door, since removed, led directly from outside. White was one of the founders of the bank.

THE TIRRELL-NEVIN HOUSE. This home was owned by shoe manufacturer Minot Tirrell and later by the Honorable Edward B. Nevin, who represented Weymouth in the House of Representatives and the Senate. Nevin's widow later donated the property as a site for the school that was named after her husband. In 1981, the school was demolished and replaced by the Nevin Professional Building at 851 Main Street.

SOUTH SHORE HOSPITAL. On May 22, 1922, the hospital opened as Weymouth Hospital in this building, formerly the home of H.B. Reed, a noted and respected shoe manufacturer. The hospital offered 22 beds, a sterile operating room, a delivery room, a nursery, and even an x-ray machine. In 1967, the building was replaced by a larger one.

THE NASH STORE. The William G. Nash Store, in Liberty Square (at the corner of Main and West Streets), sold groceries, medicines, farm tools, and paint. Capt. Thomas Nash's house is on the right. William Nash opened his grocery store in 1834 and lived upstairs for 72 years. When he died at age 94, he was the oldest active grocer in the United States.

THE CADY HOME. From left to right are Benjamin Cady, Mary (Loud) Cady, Maria (Loud) Lewis, Lizzie Cady, and Anna Cady in front of their home at 58 West Street, which is now divided into apartments.

THE STETSON SHOE FACTORY. The factory stretched along Main Street near the intersection with West Street in 1930. The white house on the corner of Main and Middle Streets, on the far left, was Mrs. Wilcox's boardinghouse and cafe. Most of the other houses on Main Street have now been replaced by businesses, including a bank and a car wash. On the left-hand side of West Street are Thomas Nash's barn and carriage house. At the lower edge of the

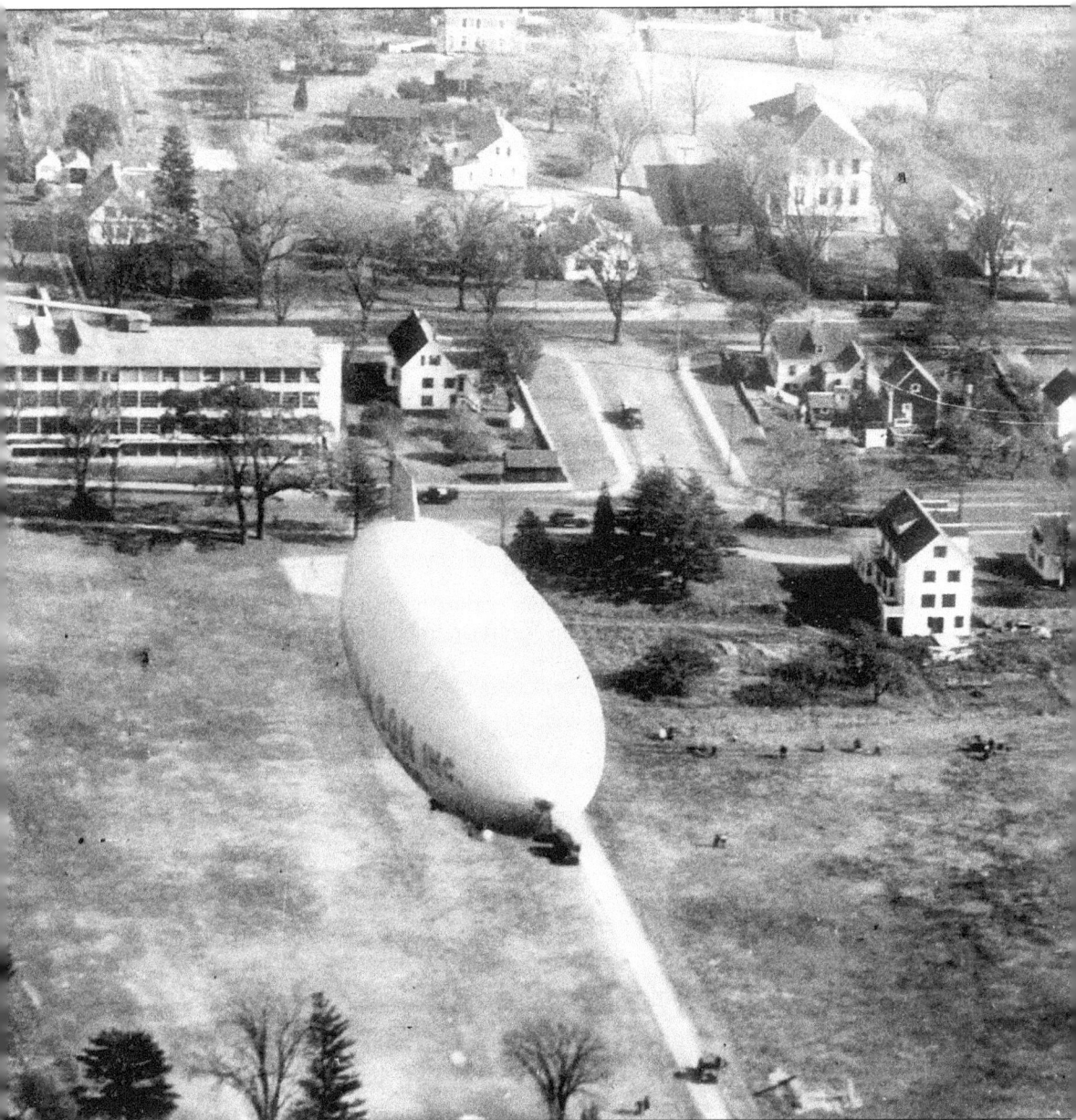

photograph, on the left, is a white house belonging to songwriter Billy Hill, which is now the site of a Baptist church. Billy Hill, hailed as "America's modern Stephen Foster," wrote film scores for Paramount, MGM, and Columbia Studios. He composed *Have You Ever Been Lonely*, *Chapel in the Moonlight*, *Empty Saddles*, and *The Last Roundup*, popularized by stars such as Bing Crosby and Gene Autry. More recently, *The Glory of Love* was a hit for Bette Midler.

GERTRUDE AND CHARLES HALL. Shown in front of their home at 26 Elm Street (now No. 34) c. 1908, these two children had been born in Whitman to Nathaniel and Mary Hall.

THE OLD COLONY RAILROAD. The Old Colony Railroad carried passengers from Boston to Cape Cod via this station on Pond Street in South Weymouth from 1845 until 1959. John M. Whitcomb was the depot master.

THE WATERWORKS. The Weymouth Water Works was built in 1885 on Hollis Street using red brick and a slate roof. The main water intake went from Great Pond along the rail line to the Hollis Street Pumping Station. The pumping station was a steam-powered plant; a separate building behind the station housed the coal. By 1895, the commissioners reported that the waterworks served 2,183 homes, with 2,948 faucets, 298 water closets, and 219 bathtubs. A whistle installed on the roof sounded the alert for events such as school cancellations, fires, or children lost in the woods. George Sargent, the man on the left in the picture below, was an engineer who gave tours of the waterworks to schoolchildren.

JASON AND CAROLINE (WHITE) HOLBROOK. Holbrook (1810–1892), a shoemaker and farmer, and Mrs. Holbrook (1806–1882) were the great-great-grandparents of actor Hal Holbrook. The Holbrook family is directly descended from Thomas Holbrook, who came to Weymouth with Reverend Hull's company in 1635. Thomas Holbrook was a signer of the original land grant of the town.

THE HOLBROOK HOUSE BRICK WALK. Weymouth Historical Society member Jim Palmieri puts the finishing touches on the walk, which incorporates more than 150 bricks engraved with the names of individuals chosen by sponsors who purchased bricks to support the society. The grounds of the Holbrook House also feature a memorial to Pvt. William A. Torrey of the 7th U.S. Cavalry, who perished on June 25, 1876, at Little Big Horn under the command of Gen. George Armstrong Custer. A picture of the Holbrook House appears on page 6.

THE NATHANIEL SHAW ESTATE. This home stood at 696 Main Street in South Weymouth until it was replaced by an office building now occupied by Eye Health Services. Nathaniel Shaw (1804–1860) inherited a thriving shoe business from his father, Capt. Nathaniel Shaw. He not only transformed the business into a major enterprise but also became renowned for his prominence in civic and church affairs and for founding a bank. Despite his business acumen, he was also known for his congeniality; one colleague commented that he seemed to "carry sunshine with him wherever he went."

Four

EAST WEYMOUTH

COMMERCIAL STREET. This part of Jackson Square has changed little since this photograph was taken *c*. 1870, although paving and streetlights have been added. On the right is 1282 Commercial Street. The large building at the back, after suffering badly in a fire, became a single-story building that now houses professional offices.

JACKSON SQUARE. Along the north side of Jackson Square, the building on the far left was the home of H.A. Tirrell. The building in the center housed C.F. Stetson's shoe store, Rich's dry goods, and barber Charles Scott. The building on the right housed Merchant's tailoring and Grover's drugstore on the ground floor, with Merchant's residence upstairs and Connell's barbershop in the basement.

OLD HOME WEEK. In August 1912, Weymouth spent an entire week in celebration. Stores and the bandstand in Jackson Square were bedecked with patriotic bunting and banners, and electric lights were strung up. Children lined the curbs eagerly awaiting the parade of bands and floats. Another view of the bandstand appears on page 74.

BROAD STREET, LOOKING WEST. On the left is the steeple of the Methodist Episcopal church and a home next door where the Weymouth House of Pizza stands today, as well as a small Cape Cod–style house that is now part of Toma's Appliances. On the right is Haskell's Boot Factory and the original Church of the Immaculate Conception, both of which were replaced by a church and parking lot. The Greek Revival house next door still stands on the corner of Cottage Street, behind a bank.

GARDNER BLOCK. This block on Commercial Street in Jackson Square housed E.G. Gardner, which offered dry and fancy goods; Ford and Phillips, which sold furniture, children's carriages, lamps, and similar items; and W.H. Spencer, which sold stoves and tinware. Gardner's offices were upstairs. The house on the right was moved around the corner to Pleasant Street to make room to build the Weymouth Light & Power store; the Gardner block was razed to build the East Weymouth post office.

WEYMOUTH LIGHT & POWER. Next to the Gardner Block, at the corner of Pleasant Street, the Weymouth Light & Power store offered laborsaving appliances for home, office, store, or factory, advertising, "All work done by skilled artisans." The building, at 1373 Commercial Street, was later used by several other businesses and as a welfare office but is now vacant.

JACKSON SQUARE. In the late 1800s, the west side of the square featured the home of the Bicknell family and Sylvester's Market (previously called Rice's Market); the latter was torn down in 1939. Jackson Square Auto and George Washington Toma now occupy this site at 1353 Commercial Street.

PEASLEE LOCK. In the late 1800s, this versatile enterprise at 1436 Pleasant Street included not only locksmith services but also a gunsmith, an electrician, a paint store, and a bicycle repair shop. The building later housed Jackson Square Paint and is now occupied by Ford Florist.

JUSTICE HARDWARE. Arthur Justice (shown here greeting a future customer) opened his hardware store at 782 Broad Street in 1939 and sold hardware, kitchenware, seeds, fertilizers, garden tools, paint, and insecticides. He later moved the business across the street to 827 Broad Street and, in 1953, sold it to Benjamin DiBona. The DiBona family still runs the business.

BROAD STREET. Jackson Square businesses along Broad Street in 1885 included the drugstore of E.G. Cutter, the Weymouth Clothing Store, the post office, and F.B. Reed's jewelry store, with a savings bank upstairs. In the background are the steeples of the Methodist church and Immaculate Conception Catholic Church.

THE ODD FELLOWS BUILDING. Built in 1889 at 1245 Commercial Street, at the corner of Cottage Street, the building still stands, although its top floor was removed in 1962. The second floor is still used for functions, and the first floor is occupied by Dave MacDonald's South Shore Hobby Shop. The steeple in the background, at the top of the Methodist church, was brought down by Hurricane Carol in 1954.

WEYMOUTH HIGH SCHOOL AND TOWN HALL. This aerial view from August 1938 shows Weymouth High School and the Weymouth Town Hall. The center portion of the high school was completed in 1898. Separate wings with classrooms and the boys' and girls' gymnasiums were constructed during the 1920s, as was the town hall, on the right. The high school burned down in 1971 after being used as a junior high school for many years. It was replaced by a new building that houses the Abigail Adams Intermediate School. The War Memorial Wall, stretching across the front of the lawn, originally commemorated Weymouth residents who died in World War I but, sadly, has had to expand its scope.

LEGION FIELD. Legion Memorial Field was once a mosquito-infested swamp, but the American Legion Post contributed $8,000 for draining and filling the field and constructing the front gate. This 1938 view, looking southeast toward Chard Street, shows the dump at Libby Field and the Strong & Garfield Shoe Factory. The field includes two baseball diamonds, two football gridirons, two grandstands (with seating for 2,700), seven tennis courts, a quarter-mile track, jumping pits, a field house, a broadcasting booth, and parking for 1,000 cars.

WHITMAN'S POND. Shown, from left to right, are Edward F. Hanley, Mrs. Frances H. Hanley, Mrs. Calvin Crocker, and Mrs. C. Mason. (The children are unidentified.) This section of the pond—seen from Lakeshore Drive, looking toward the current site of the Lakeview Manor housing project—was once the site of Col. William Castle's apple orchard. A dam built for the Rolling Mill at the ironworks doubled the size of Whitman's Pond and covered the apple tree stumps that can be seen behind the men and women in the photograph. The stumps were exposed when the water level dropped during a drought in 1949.

CLAPP MEMORIAL. Mr. and Mrs. Edwin Clapp built the David Clapp Memorial in 1903 in memory of their son, who had died the year before. The gymnasium, bowling alley, reading room, and outdoor sports area supported the memorial's purpose of promoting physical, social, intellectual, and spiritual welfare.

HOUSE ROCK. The fun-loving Weymouth Historical Society poses under this "perched" boulder, which is alternately known as the Sphinx, Watching Rock, or Queen Rock. Some imagine that they can see Queen Victoria's profile, facing east toward Britain, while others see Barney the dinosaur. Measuring 42 feet long, 30 feet wide, and 37 feet high, the rock is certainly larger than many houses in Weymouth.

BROAD STREET. The trolley line ran from South Weymouth Depot along Pleasant Street to Jackson Square. It then turned up Broad Street and continued to the carbarn at Central Square. After 40 years of service, these trolleys ceased operation on December 16, 1933. The carbarn was later used by the Hudson Bus Company. Each trolley was staffed by a motorman and a conductor. In 1902, the men worked 10 hours each day, seven days per week, for pay of $14 per week.

LOVELL'S CORNER. The Chalke family had a grocery store at 1159 Washington Street near Lovell's corner (at the intersection of Washington Street and Mutton Lane, formerly known as Pleasant Street). The store was recently torn down, but the building behind it, originally a fire station, still stands as Carroll's Printing.

THE TRAIN STATION. The East Weymouth stop on the South Shore Railroad, later the Old Colony Railroad, was built at the end of Station Street and offered streetcar connections to Nantasket Beach. The station burned on February 24, 1972.

RANDALL'S GROVE. In August 1893, the "Inasmuch Circle" of King's Daughters held a Friday evening picnic supper in Randall's Grove, where "the ladies learned that a pleasant outing can be had near home," according to the *Weymouth Gazette*. After feasting on steamed clams, corn, and pastry, they posed for this photograph, taken by David Randall.

GAREYS' VIEW. From their home at 45 Randall Avenue, the Gareys saw the Canterbury and Haskells shoe factory on the left, the Immaculate Conception Church in the center, and the Canterbury family home and stables to the right of the church.

IMMACULATE CONCEPTION CHURCH. Constructed at a cost of $30,000, primarily by parishioners who worked 10 to 12 hours per day, the church was dedicated on November 23, 1879. Masses were said in the basement before the completion of the upper part of the church, which had a capacity of 700. The building was razed in June 1967 after the new church and parish center were built.

JACKSON SQUARE. The Weymouth town band presented open-air concerts during warm weather at this bandstand in Jackson Square, also shown on page 60. Behind the bandstand in this view looking southeast is Peak's Block, where the East Weymouth Life newspaper offices were located. Beyond that block is the steeple of the Washington School.

THE IRONWORKS FLOOD. In 1887, floodwaters spilled over the Whitman's Pond Dam, coursing down Pleasant Street below the old police station, wiping out the roadway and exposing the sewer pipe. The gambrel-roofed building on the left was the early-19th-century home of David Rice. In 1822, Rice's son Urban had established Weymouth's first Methodist organization in this house.

HENRY VOGEL. Henry Vogel, shown here in front of his home at 121 Cedar Street in 1886, was Weymouth's last surviving Civil War veteran. He died in 1944 at the age of 97. Every Memorial Day, he stood on the front lawn to review the parade and receive homage from the participants.

BELLAIRE. Built by Peter W. French in 1890 at 1772 Commercial Street, this mansion was razed in 1967 to make way for a 10-home subdivision. For several years, the barn housed the Dressco Belting Company. The ledge in the right foreground was leveled and used to build a wall across the front of the property.

LONG HILL. This view from Long Hill over Grove Street toward Pleasant and Shawmut Streets shows the old Weymouth Iron Company (the large dark building on the left) and the East Weymouth Congregational Church (often called the Old White Church) on the extreme right. After the church was destroyed by fire in 1903, the old police station was built on the site. That former police station is now occupied by the park department and used as a teen center.

Five

EDUCATION

THE ADAMS SCHOOL. Named for Abigail Adams because it was located near her birthplace, the Adams School was a two-room schoolhouse built in 1854. In this 1897 photograph, students in the first through fourth grades pose with their teacher, Minnie Mathewson, who was paid $475 that year.

THE TUFTS SCHOOL. The Tufts School, also known as the Mount Pleasant School, was built at the corner of Richmond and Keith Streets before 1871 and was used as a primary and intermediate school until it was replaced by the new Hunt School in 1915. The school had central heating but no electricity.

POND SCHOOL TEACHERS. The school's teachers c. 1930 were, from left to right, Nellie Beaton (grade seven), Esther Visco (grade five), Myrtle Pray (grade four), Isabella Dacey (grade three), Ralph Stewart (grade six), Alice Fulton (grade eight), Josephine Ray (grade two), and Dorothy Fitzpatrick (grade one). Fulton also served as principal. In 1964, during Fulton's final year of teaching, the Parent-Teacher Association voted to rename the school in her honor.

POND SCHOOL STUDENTS. The second-grade class of 1937–1938 included, from left to right, the following: (front row) Joan Austin, Janice Rathgeb, Helen McGlynn, Joanne Monahan, Elaine Anderson, Eva Murphy, Marielle Simpson, Olive Stackpole, Jane MacGoldrick, Jean Baghdalian, and June Kenney; (middle row) Charles Barielo, Wendell Gassett, Emilie Ann Skiffington, Judith Anderson, Mary Lou Stevenson, Phoebe Stockwell, Janet Mitchell, John Mandell, and Charles Stebbins; (back row) Robert Marr, Jack MacDonald, David McCarthy, Donald Ferguson, Arthur Emberly, Carl Olson, Robert Merten, Joseph Griffin, Donald Cole, and Harry Thompson.

THE FRANKLIN SCHOOLHOUSE. Built at the corner of Broad and Putnam Streets in 1897 at a cost of $13,000, the schoolhouse had four rooms: two for grammar school students, one for intermediate students, and one for primary students. Classes were large: in 1885, the enrollment was 225, an average of 56 students per room. The building was torn down sometime before 1930 to make way for the Central Fire Station.

NEW HOUSING, 1950. As veterans from World War II started their families, the demand for housing in the Boston area soared; Weymouth and neighboring communities began evolving into bedroom suburbs, where most residents worked in the distant city. In just three years (1947–1949), more than 1,000 homes were built, and school enrollments were expected to grow by 60 to 70 percent during the 1950s.

THE McCULLOCH SCHOOL. The McCulloch School on Green Street was one of several schools built in the 1950s and 1960s in response to the town's rapidly growing population. It opened in 1959, closed in 1981, and is now the Whipple Senior Center. One of the two first-grade classes in 1962 included, from left to right, the following: (first row) Richard Cronk, Stephen Materia, and Joseph Sweeney; (second row) Patty King, Nancy MacCallum, Peggy McLellan, Debbie Sargent, unidentified, unidentified, Debbie Mahon, and Karen Naughton; (third row) Michael Devine, Michael Lawson, Karen Ericson, Debbie Tirrell, unidentified, Marie Decoste, Kim Gatey, Jim Tagg, and Michael Mahoney; (fourth row) Kevin Cavanaugh, Michael Joseph, Daniel Winters, teacher Louise Fredericks, William Lockhead, Richard Veautrineau, and Joseph Yoder.

THE HOWE SCHOOL. South High School was established in the vestry of the Union Congregational Church in 1865, moved to Rogers Hall, and then occupied this building from 1875 until it merged with the newer high school that was built in 1898 to serve the entire town. Named for prominent physician Appleton Howe, the school was located on Torrey Street, where Old South Union Church now has a parking lot.

THE WEYMOUTH HIGH SCHOOL FOOTBALL TEAM, 1895. Since the town had two high schools, it drew its team from both: eight members were from South High School and three from North. Shown, from left to right, are the following: (front row) Percy Baker, Holly Morales, Charles Whelan, Thomas Reidy, Andrew Burrell, and Arthur Hunt; (back row) Joseph Manion, William Bentley, John Hart, Ernest Thayer, and Cornelius Tirrell.

WEYMOUTH HIGH SCHOOL. Before its two side wings were added in the 1920s, Weymouth High School consisted of this single building, constructed in 1898 with an appropriation of $50,000. Enrollment during its opening year was 239 students. By 1923, enrollment had soared to 560 students, and the school had to be divided into morning and afternoon sessions, despite the addition of a two-room "portable schoolhouse."

THE FOOTBALL TEAM. The undefeated Weymouth High School football team of 1936 included, from left to right, the following: (front row) Stan Lukis, Harry Botterud, Russ Johnson, Bob Pirie, Al DiLorenzo, John Quirk, and Mark Hanabury; (back row) Al Wilder, Bob Spear, Jim Stevens, and Art Wilder.

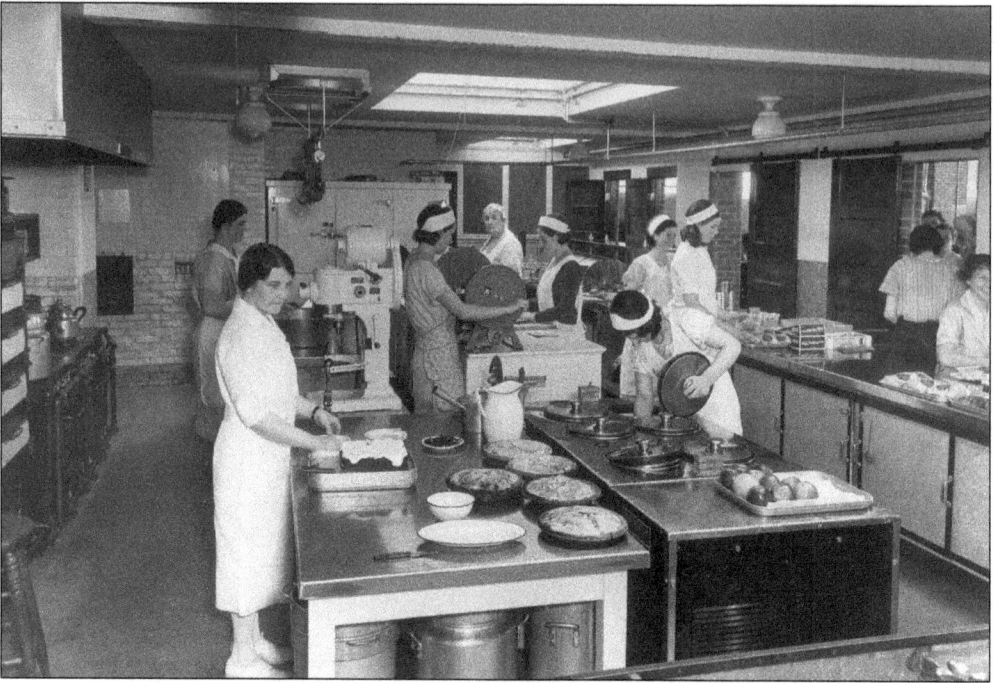

THE CAFETERIA. In the early 1930s, Eva Skala taught the girls at Weymouth High School how to cook, sew, and keep house in her domestic science class. She also presided over the cafeteria in the basement of the old high school.

THE WEYMOUTH HIGH SCHOOL BAND. In 1944, the band members included, from left to right, the following: (front row) K. Madden, D. Beckes, W. Smith, R. Casey, R. Nelson, P. MacKinnon, E. Regan, F. Parsons, S. Shepherd, R. Steele, and B. Hearn; (middle row) J. Burke, R. Nelson, M. Walsh, R. King, C. Stone, D. Resnick, C. McKenzie, and R. Lyons; (back row) F. Whalen, M. Eddy, band director J. Calderwood, A. Sheehan, and P. McCarthy.

84

SENIOR PLAY. In May 1942, the senior class presented the three-act play *All About Eve*, a comedy about the efforts of a high school newspaper editor to keep girls off the staff. Cast members included, from left to right, the following: (front row) D. Shirley, M. Gerrior, R. Dondero, E. Gaskill, M. Dizer, G. Jones, J. Connell, and E. Morse; (back row) E. McIsaac, T. Roberts, R. Sargent, Z. Alemian, D. Jackson, D. Watson, E. Yetman, and S. Hall.

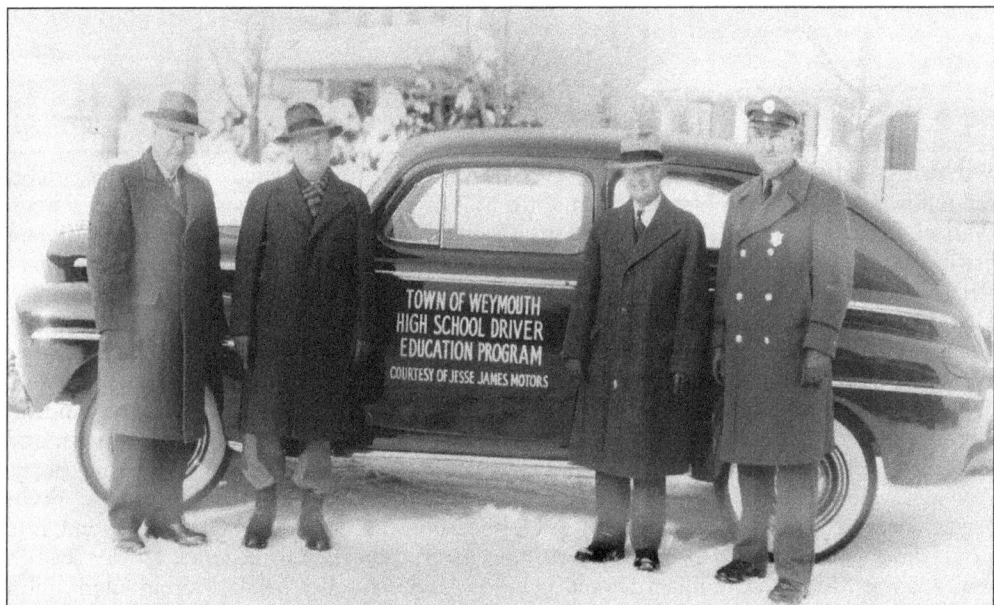

DRIVER'S EDUCATION. In the mid-1940s, this vehicle was the pride of the driver's education program at Weymouth High School. Posing with the car are, from left to right, Harold Olson (assistant superintendent of schools), Elmer Mapes (superintendent), Jesse James (who donated the car), and an unidentified police officer.

WEYMOUTH HIGH SCHOOL FACULTY, 1951. Faculty members include, from left to right, the following: (first row) Hilmer Nelson, Otto Mahn, Waldo Swan, George Klay, Ray Parker, Wallace Whittle (principal), Thomas Lyons, George Nott, Fred Carlson, Leo Hayes, William Erwin, Joseph Whittemore, and Harold Nelson; (second row) Laura Nash, Helen Lyons, Mary Arnold, Louise Hill, Jane Tower, Mary Gloster, Alice White, Olive Hackett, Dorothy Murphy, Dorothy MacGregor, Helen Norris, Virginia Nye, and Anita Petrucci; (third row) Russell Jack, Claire Heaver, Ruth Mayo, Marie Ghiorse, Dorothy Pearson, Elizabeth Waterman, Esther Benson, Martha Vining, Jean Young, Edna Flaherty, Elizabeth Palmer, Herberta Stockwell, and Harry Arlanson; (fourth row) Eva Skala, Lousie Masters, Alice Fay, Polyanna Andem, Dorothy Driscoll, Ernestine Canning, Helena Reidy, Elizabeth Rogers, Evelyn Silvester, and Oral Page; (fifth row) John Ghiorse, Walter Gutterson, Margaret Langford, Arthur Scott, Alvah Raymond, and Philip Henley; (sixth row) John Gannon, Richard Whitmore, Ervin Stuart, Prescott Brown, Francis Martin, and John Collins; (seventh row) Clarence Lyond, Eric Roy, Jalmar Nelson, Lewis Bacon, Robert Lang, James Steele, and Frederick Hoyle; (eighth row) George McCarthy, William Dwyer, James Boland, Russell Mazzola, Harold Clark, John Delahunt, and Paul Cleaves.

Six

RECREATION

HERRING RUN. Every spring, crowds line the banks of the "Herring Brook" on Commercial Street to watch the herring make their annual pilgrimage upstream from the Atlantic Ocean to their spawning grounds in Whitman's Pond. At the time this photograph was taken in the 1930s, the fish were being transported in barrels from this point to the pond. In 1947, the town obtained funding to build a herring run. In recent years, the herring have made such a comeback that more than one million may use the run each day.

THE NORFOLK CYCLE CLUB. The club, named for Norfolk County, in which Weymouth is located, had rooms in the Fogg Opera House in Columbian Square in South Weymouth. In addition to bicycle races, they sponsored dances, minstrel shows, and a banjo and guitar club. This bicycle was made especially for the Brockton Fair.

THE WOMEN'S CHRISTIAN TEMPERANCE UNION (WCTU). The temperance crusade of 1874 saw one of the largest memberships of any women's society in the world. The women of the WCTU furnished entertainment, social suppers, and maintained rooms "on Pleasant Street" (possibly at the Fogg Opera House) as a place for reading and recreation.

THE NORFOLK CLUB. In 1890, local youth excited about the freedom accorded by the newly invented bicycle formed the Norfolk Cycle Club and established quarters in the Fogg Opera House. By 1898, the group had grown to 85 members and incorporated as the Norfolk Club. As the center of cycling interest in Weymouth (and other towns in Norfolk County), the club sponsored races against rival clubs from nearby towns. Even into the 1920s, when sporting interest in cycling began to flag, the club prospered as a social club, acquiring title to the Fogg Opera House and limiting its membership numbers.

THE CAMP FIRE GIRLS, 1916. Accompanied by their guardian, Effie Chandler, and the Reverend Fred Line, the girls of the Miss-a-hickon Group pose in front of the South Weymouth Universalist Church on Mother's Day in 1916. The girls are, from left to right, as follows: (front row) Lillian Carley (married name, Pelrine), Ardell Shepherd (Doble), and Evelyn Howe (Marigott); (middle row) Alice Gay (Ripley), Marjorie Thomas (Chisholm), Ruth Benson, and Elsie Thomas (Dodge); (back row) Doris Churchill (Muir), Eleanor Sherman (Montgomery), and Helen Line, the daughter of Reverend Line.

CAMP FIRE GIRLS. This group of Camp Fire Girls, the first in Weymouth, was organized in 1913 by Maria Hawes of Pleasant Street in South Weymouth. Before being disbanded three years later, the group posed in the back of Woodrock Farm in the Lovell's Corner area. From left to right are the following: (front row) Alta Hawes (Cole), Alice Forsyth, Mabel Devine (Boisclair), and Lulu Tisdale (Murphy); (back row) Florence Devine (Corbett), Marjorie Rae (Hughes), Ardice White (Sample), Edith Smith (Charlwood), Ray Sprague (Damon), and Helen White (Thompson). Accompanying the girls is Nellie Brewster, wearing an impressive hat.

THE STETSON BAND. Sponsored by the Stetson Shoe Company, the band is seen here in front of Clapp Hall participating in a parade in Lincoln Square on June 19, 1914. Note the tracks of the Weymouth Street Railway on Broad Street.

FOURTH OF JULY PARADE, 1913. This float, sponsored by the Dorothea Dix Tent of the Daughters of Veterans, won third prize. The house in the background is 16 Cottage Street in East Weymouth; the steeple of the original Immaculate Conception Church can be seen behind a telephone pole, on the left.

PRIZEWINNING PATRIOTS. The Town of Weymouth awarded prizes in several categories to organizations that participated in the tercentenary parade, in 1923. The Hunt School won second place in the "best school participation" category for their portrayal of the Revolutionary period in Weymouth.

THE COLUMBIAN FIFE AND DRUM CORPS. Established in July 1896, the Fife and Drum Corps raised funds from the townspeople to acquire their bass drum and cymbals. They performed at public events such as political rallies and fire musters, appearing at the Conqueror Veteran Fire Association at the Fairgrounds in September 1896. The group was discontinued after their exhibition on Armistice Day in 1918.

THE STANLEY STEAMER. Quiet, smokeless, and capable of great speeds, the Stanley Steamer became a popular early automobile. At the wheel of this example is Arthur C. Heald, accompanied by Charles Willets in the front seat and H.S. Stetson and an unidentified man in the back.

THE WEYMOUTH FAIRGROUNDS. Established for the purpose of improving and encouraging agriculture and horticulture, the Weymouth Agricultural and Industrial Society operated an annual fair, with events that included horse racing, clay pigeon shoots, and the judging of produce, livestock, and crafts, from 1864 until 1972.

So. Weymouth Agricultural Fair
1904

THE MOBILE SHOE SHOP. Wilbur Loud took this "10-footer" shoe shop to the Weymouth Fair on an oxcart in 1904. The shop was typical of the structures where the Weymouth shoemaking industry had its beginnings. It was used as a trade display and won first prize.

MEMORIAL DAY RACES. Races were held on Memorial Day at the fairgrounds in South Weymouth, but the racetrack, built for trotters, was unsuited to automobiles. After an accident in 1940, a 15-year-old boy, Johnny Wright, was seriously injured. He was struck by one of the racecars as he dashed across the track to see the fire caused by the accident. This incident, combined with complaints that the festivities disrupted Memorial Day ceremonies in a nearby cemetery, led to popular demands that the races be discontinued.

KRAMER'S HAYLOFT. In 1959, Sam Kramer converted his dairy barn on Union Street into a square dance hall, noting that "square-dancing and drinking do not mix." Lessons and dances for teens and adults provided wholesome entertainment.

THE WEYMOUTH ARENA. Built in 1953 by Gus Salt, the arena on Middle Street grew from a roofless shed into a structure that was open even in midsummer, accommodating 800 to 1,000 skaters each week for hockey, figure skating, and public recreation. The rink was purchased by Ed Dalton in 1967 and burned to the ground in 1975.

96

Solve Your Summer Evening's Entertainment Problem at the

Drive-In Theatre Weymouth

SIT IN YOUR CAR
SEE AND HEAR MOVIES

Last SHOW 10:30 P.M.

ENTER OR LEAVE AT ANY TIME

ROUTE 3A, South Shore
One Mile South of the New Fore River Bridge

Elderly people, invalids, fat people and tall people may enjoy the show in comfort and privacy without leaving their cars.

Bring the family and even household pets if you wish!

ADMISSION

35¢

Per Person

CHILDREN Under 10 Admitted FREE.

No Charge For Car

Cont'd nightly Rain or Shine — Show starts 8:15
LAST SHOW at 10:30 P.M.

THE WEYMOUTH DRIVE-IN. The first open-air theater in New England opened on Route 3A in Weymouth on May 28, 1936. This advertisement from 1938 targets those who avoided ordinary indoor theaters. Six uniformed concession boys catered to the cars with hand-held baskets of tonic, popcorn, and candy. In 1965, the owners expanded the 8 acres to 22 and added two screens, a playground, and a concession stand. Electric car heaters enabled the drive-in to stay open all year. Despite all these improvements and enticements, the drive-in closed in 1976.

THE WEYMOUTH BRAVES. In the 1930s, Weymouth had a semiprofessional baseball team, the Braves. They played at local parks against teams like St. Ann's of Quincy, the West Quincy Mohawks, Bayside Athletic Club of Hull, and the South Quincy Cubs. Team members include, from left to right, the following: (front row) Bob Nelson, Jim Pica, Ray Leary, Scotty Weir, G. Harrington, and Leo Quinlan; (back row) John Fraher, Russ Rose, Tom Dwyer, John Harrington (with Billy Thurston in front of him), and Jerry Dwyer.

KICKBALL CHAMPS. The members of the 1959 champion kickball team from Mosquito Plain Park on Century Road display their trophies. From left to right are the following: (front row) Kathy McCone, Claudette Clarke, Sandra Richardson, Sally McIver, Maryanne Laffey, Dianne Clarke, and Barbara Cheney; (back row) Regina Clarke, Dianne Duarte, Sue Markhard, instructor Sarah Gallahue, park commissioner Dave Kelly, Pat Dempsey, and Ruthie Cronin.

WESSAGUSSETT WATER CARNIVAL. The Weymouth Park Department sponsored the water carnival at Wessagussett Beach in 1953. The younger boys shown are participating in a race that was one of 22 events.

WATER BALLERINAS. Pausing during their preparations for the Water Carnival at Wessagussett Beach are, from left to right, Karen Smith, Leslie Main, instructor Merry Lewis, Dorothy Pitts, and Linda Smith. The program had been planned for mid-August but had to be postponed until September 3 because of water pollution. Dorothy Pitts Miller is now the assistant principal at the William Seach School.

SENIOR CITIZENS' OUTING. In April 1958, Weymouth seniors dressed up for an outing to the Cinerama Theater in Boston. Standing outside the bus are, from left to right, the following: (front row) Mrs. Tucker, Mrs. Byam, Mrs. Greers, Mrs. Regan (a visiting nurse), Mrs. Bonardi (a visiting nurse), Mrs. Robbins, Mrs. Smith, and Mrs. Lynch; (back row) Eleanor Lane and Mrs. Connors.

CHECKERS IN THE PARK. Charles Turner (left) contemplates his checkers strategy at the Weymouth Senior Citizens Picnic, held at Weston Park in observance of Senior Citizens Week in September 1960. Margaret V. Spillane and Catherine Meier watch Turner and Walter L. Walsh.

Seven

MILITARY

SOLDIERS' MONUMENT. After the tercentenary procession on June 16, 1923, a wreath was placed at the Soldiers' Monument by veterans of each war in which Weymouth soldiers have participated or by their descendants. The adults shown are, from left to right, David Dunbar (Civil War), Emery E. Welch (Spanish-American War), and William A. Connell (World War I). The children who represent ancestors are Richard Edson Mathewson (War of 1812), second from the left; Louis Dent Bradford (King Philip's War); Frederic Gilbert Bauer Jr. (French and Indian War); and Ronald Graydon Torrey (Revolutionary War). (It has not been determined which of the last three boys is which.)

GEN. JAMES L. BATES. In 1849, abandoning a career as a teacher in the Weymouth public schools, Bates joined a stock company and sailed in the *Edward Everett* around Cape Horn to seek his fortune in the California Gold Rush. A year later, having found no gold, Bates joined a group of shareholders who bought out the others and brought the ship back to Boston. When the Civil War began, he was instrumental in forming Weymouth men into Company H, which became part of the 12th Regiment of Massachusetts. Commissioned as captain of Company H on April 29, 1861, he rapidly rose to the rank of major and was promoted to colonel and to the command of the 12th Regiment in September 1862. Despite being wounded on the first day of the Battle of Gettysburg, he remained with his regiment and was mustered out of service in 1865 after coming under fire 28 times. In 1868, he was commissioned a brevet-brigadier general on the basis of his Civil War service.

THE REYNOLDS POST, GRAND ARMY OF THE REPUBLIC (GAR). Post 58 of the GAR, formed on July 14, 1868, was named for Gen. John F. Reynolds of the 1st Army Corps. Reynolds led the 12th Massachusetts Infantry and was killed on the first day of the Battle of Gettysburg. Located on Commercial Street across from Station Street, the hall had been a schoolhouse and was donated to the veterans. When it burned on February 24, 1939, some of the precious Civil War mementos were rescued.

PVT. JEREMIAH QUINN. A member of Company H of the 4th Massachusetts Cavalry, Quinn was taken prisoner on January 1, 1863, and spent time in Andersonville and Libby Prisons. Nevertheless, he was the first Union soldier in Richmond after the surrender, pulling down the rebel flag and raising the Union flag over that city on April 3, 1865.

CIVIL WAR VETERANS. About 250 veterans from Post 58 of the Grand Army of the Republic gathered at Thomas Corner in North Weymouth (at the intersection of North and Sea Streets) to make their annual visit to the graves of their fallen comrades. From North Weymouth, an elegant array of carriages filled with soldiers proceeded around the town to decorate the graves. At Mount Hope Cemetery, the companies were massed in battalion form to have their picture taken on May 30, 1882.

HENRY VOGEL. At his home in the early 1940s, Vogel (Weymouth's oldest Civil War veteran) is greeted by Al Perette Sr., a veteran of World War I. The tall man in the center is William Seach Jr., a survivor of the attack on Pearl Harbor. In front of Seach is his father, who was a veteran of World War I and the Boxer Rebellion and was one of Weymouth's five Medal of Honor winners. Another picture of Vogel appears on page 75.

WEYMOUTH TERCENTENARY. More than 4,000 people participated in the parade that marked Weymouth's tercentenary in June 1923. This photograph, taken at the corner of Lincoln and North Streets, shows the U.S. Naval Band.

BLIMPS AT THE NAVAL AIR STATION. After the South Weymouth Naval Air Station was commissioned on March 1, 1942, blimps patrolled the Atlantic coast, protecting Allied convoys by spotting enemy submarines. When each blimp went out, three or four carrier pigeons were taken along, to send messages back to the base, because subs could hear radio signals. During the 1950s and 1960s, the station had a squadron of N Class all-weather airships that replaced the K Class ships used during World War II. These modern blimps of 1955 had continuous patrol capabilities and were able to detect incoming enemy submarines.

THE *K-SHIP* BLIMP. While a team of sailors mans ropes to help stabilize this blimp in the mid-1950s, another sailor relays directions to the sailor at the top of the mooring mast.

THE SOUTH WEYMOUTH NAVAL AIR STATION. The building at the bottom of the picture housed the enlisted men's club on the left side, the recreation hall in the center, and the Navy Exchange on the right. The large hangar in the upper-center was under construction in 1957 when this photograph was taken; gas-storage bunkers can be seen behind it. The buildings on the left held administrative offices. The base was closed in 1997.

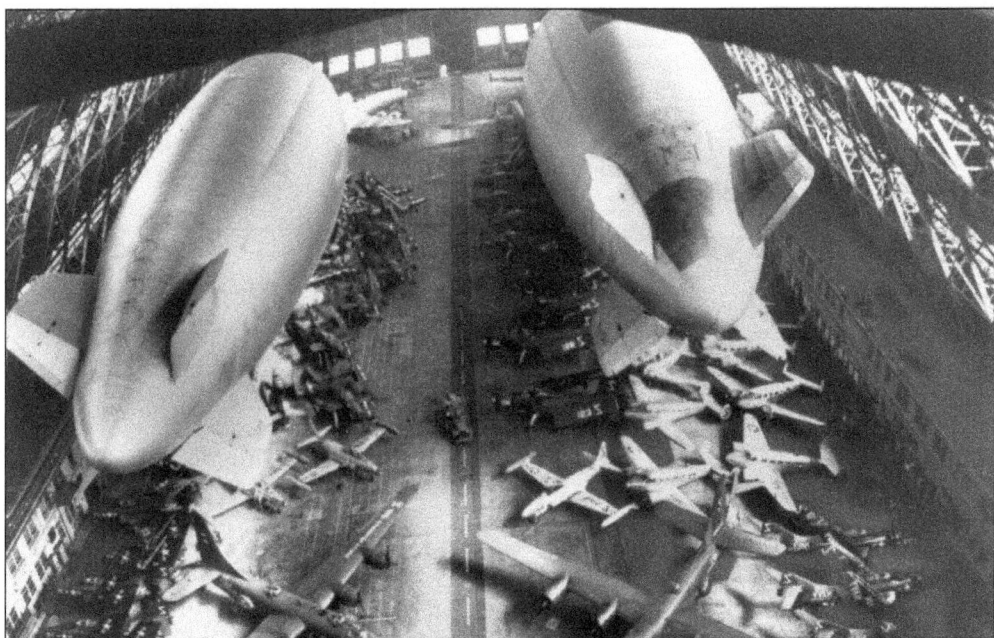

SHELTERED FROM HURRICANE CAROL. Before Hurricane Carol struck the Weymouth area on August 3, 1954, all aircraft and every naval vehicle based at the South Weymouth Naval Air Station were brought into Hangar 1. Gusts of 130 miles per hour were recorded at the Blue Hills Observatory in nearby Milton.

AIR STATION SECURITY. In the late 1950s, the staff of the South Weymouth Naval Air Station main gate on White Street, included, from left to right, William Martin, Jim Murray, Jim Campbell, Jim Zirkle, Chief William Foster, Fred Lumley, Tom Countie, unidentified, Walter Devereaux, Vincent Maloney, Bob McNeil, and Sam Williams.

AIR STATION SENTRIES. The South Weymouth Naval Air Station was closed at the end of World War II but reopened on December 4, 1953. Qualified sentries were stationed at the main gate on White Street to greet the public and secure the facility. Donald Sargent is shown on the left and Al Greco on the right.

Eight

POLICE AND FIRE

THE BUTLER FAMILY. Weymouth's second police chief, Patrick Butler, poses with his family. From left to right are the following: (front row) John Norman; Mary Ellen, Butler's wife, holding Margaret, who later served as town clerk; Butler; Butler's oldest daughter, Ellen; and George; (back row) Beatrice; Florence; Agnes; Edward; Alice; and Dorothy. On April 15, 1915, shortly after this picture was taken, Butler was killed in an automobile accident after 35 years with the Weymouth Police Department, including two years as chief. Butler's son Edward later became Weymouth's fourth police chief, and son John became a lieutenant. George also joined the police force; Alice and Irene married police officers. Beatrice's son George Shanahan became the Weymouth Police Department's school attendance officer, and her grandson Thomas H. Higgins became police chief in 1984.

THE POLICE STATION. In 1912, the town appropriated funds to build a new police headquarters. The new station on Pleasant Street was opened in 1914 by Chief Patrick Butler. Usually, one daytime officer or one nighttime officer was on duty, but with the increase in auto travel, it became necessary to have several officers on Sundays and holidays during the summer. A new police station was built next door in 1936.

RUM RUNNERS. Chief Edward Butler poses triumphantly with Tom Quinn, the night watchman at Stone & Webster, and Sgt. George W. Hunt in front of a "rum runner" truck that they captured at the Edison dock in 1926.

110

MOTORCYCLE PARADE. This photograph from *c.* 1931 shows Officer Kelso leading a contingent of boy scouts. A motorcycle officer had been added to the police force in 1920 to enforce traffic rules and to discourage speeding. From a police point of view, this was once one of the most difficult problems that the department faced.

PISTOL TEAM. Weymouth's prizewinning 1928 Police Rifle and Pistol Team included, from left to right, Ambrose Boyle, Norman Butler, Dr. John Bastey, Robert Panora, and John Hutchins.

CHIEF PRATT. Weymouth's third chief of police, Arthur H. Pratt, served from 1915 until 1931. The officers behind him are, from left to right, James L. Brennan, Charles Trask, Elbert Ford, ? Litchfield, Charles Baker, Bill Gaughan, William Trask, and Thomas Fitzgerald (the retired chief).

POLICE IN 1936. Officers posing in front of the new police station are, from left to right, the following: (front row) George J. Connors, Gerald Kelso, Charles Coyle, and Ralph Smith; (back row) Francis Maguire and Rod Ells.

112

CROSSING GUARDS. Police Chief Joseph O'Kane (front, center) poses in 1967 with the town's crossing guards. From left to right are the following: (first row) Alice Tancreto, Anna Morse, Gladys Blanchard, and Lucy Naas; (second row) Eileen McDonough, Mildred Mullin, Barbara Capozzoli, and Ruth Fisher; (third row) Catherine Gibson, Madeline Clark, Margaret MacDonald, Mary Mulveyhill, Jean Eldridge, and Mary Hickey; (fourth row) safety officer William Riley (known to one and all as "Officer Riley") and Capt. William Webb.

113

HOSE NO. 3. Fire Chief J. Rupert Walsh poses with this splendid piece of fire equipment, which was purchased by the town for $479.50 in 1898. From 1898 until 1910, Walsh was a member of the Board of Engineers, which ran the fire department. The board elected him to be fire chief in 1908, 1909, and 1910.

THE "BABY CARRIAGE." In 1912, the citizens of Weymouth Landing grew impatient with the town's unwillingness to purchase any motorized fire equipment. Through local contributions and the efforts of local wheelwrights and machinists, they purchased and overhauled a Matheson car, creating the vehicle known formally as Combination No. 3, and donated it to the town.

114

Combination No. 1. In 1913, the town had only one piece of motor-driven fire apparatus, the car known as the Baby Carriage that had been donated by the concerned citizens of Weymouth Landing. After a disastrous fire destroyed the town hall, a garage, and a factory, the town decided to invest in better protection and purchased two motorized pumping engines and a combination truck from the Knox Manufacturing Company. The combination engine was kept at the Athens Street Station in North Weymouth.

COMBINATION NO. 5. Members of the Weymouth Fire Department, posing proudly with their new acquisition in January 1915, are District Chief M. O'Dowd, Capt. E.W. Gardner, 1st Lt. C.S. Curtis, 2nd Lt. D.F. Daley, clerk and treasurer B.T. Hobart, J.F. Flynn, B.T. Loud, W.B. Loud, W.P. Kennedy, W.H. Miner, J.L Brennan, W.B. Baker, R. Horace, W.B. Blanchard, J.A. Carley, E.A. Bowker, C. Leary, C.A. Vining, W.B. Nash Jr., C.W. Stone, H. Selmer, and R. Bacon.

THE WEYMOUTH FIRE DEPARTMENT. The Weymouth Fire Department volunteers pose *c.* 1888 on Broad Street near the Baptist church. Driver Jim Ford overlooks volunteers, including, from left to right, the following: (front row) Rupert Walsh, Fred Hall, Gus Leach, Walter Phillips, William Cunningham, Joe Vinal, Bert Johnson, John Bacon, Ross South, Ed Sterling, Clarence Williams, Fred Cushing, and James Pray; (back row) Frank Whitten, Gus Richmond, and Waterman Burrell.

A FIRE TRUCK. While rushing to a fire *c.* 1920, this fire truck slid off the road and down an embankment. It is not known whether anyone was hurt, but seat belts certainly would have helped. It must have been quite a cold ride in this open fire truck.

117

THE BICKNELL SCHOOL. After serving as a school for more than 60 years, the Bicknell School was sold for condominium development in 1986. During the renovations, a fire that had begun in the auditorium consumed one wing of the building. The remaining structure was successfully converted into condominiums, and townhouses were built on the site of the destroyed wing.

THE FIRE STATION THAT BURNED DOWN TWICE. Weymouth Fire Station No. 3, in Lincoln Square (at the corner of Washington and Broad Streets), went up in flames on January 21, 1929, threatening all the properties in the area. The station that burned in 1929 was a replacement for one that had burned in 1872, when the station and five other buildings were destroyed. Another view of this corner appears on page 16.

118

Nine

INDUSTRY

STETSON SNAPPY TIE GIRLS. The Stetson Shoe Company sponsored the Snappy Style Show Company, which traveled as far as Springfield, hosting shows and promoting shoe fashions and general good spirits in hotel ballrooms and at store openings. The Snappy Tie Revue performed musical numbers, based on popular tunes, that praised Snappy Tie Shoes. Charles Heald, the sales manager of the Stetson Shoe Company, personally developed this unique advertising strategy. The charming performers shown here in August 1925 are, from left to right, Alice Melville, Alice McKay, Grace Loeffler, Marion Sweet, Robert Perry, Marjorie Thomas, Lillian Vaniken, and Aina Jerpi. During World War II, the Stetson logo was changed so that it did not resemble a swastika.

THE STETSON SHOE COMPANY. Founded in 1885 by Ezra Stetson and Arthur C. Heald, the Stetson Shoe Company enjoyed a nationwide reputation for superior quality. The company worked in collaboration with the vocational department of Weymouth High School: students worked in the factory in addition to their schoolwork, enabling them to graduate with a trade. Once the largest industry in Weymouth, the factory closed in 1973.

STETSON WORKERS. When blizzards put the trolleys and Stanley Steamers out of commission, the "four-legged engine" could be relied upon. This 1920 photograph shows a group of Stetson factory workers preparing to head homeward. The house with the columns is now a bank, across the street from the former Stetson factory.

THE S.W. & E. NASH SHOE SHOP. Stephen and Erastus Nash made boots, primarily for the California trade, at this factory, which was built in 1857 at the corner of Federal and Summer Streets. The boots were shipped "around the Horn." Sometime before 1896, the Moshnichka family bought the building, planted tobacco on the farm behind the factory, and manufactured cigars.

THE SPEAR SHOE FACTORY. Samuel S. Spear had a boot and shoe factory at 664 Main Street. Spear was an agent for Hall's Patent treadle sewing machine; one can be seen in the upstairs window, dating this photograph to sometime after 1889, when Spear began to offer the machines.

ICE HARVESTING. In preparation for the warm months ahead, men harvested and stored ice from ponds such as Martin's Pond, near Torrey Street and Park Avenue West.

AN ICEHOUSE. Ice was cut from several Weymouth ponds, including Great Pond, Whitman's Pond, and Martin's Pond. During the cutting season, which lasted only four to six weeks, more than 150 men were employed to cut great blocks, which were then stored in central icehouses. A railroad spur crossed Hollis Street to Great Pond, where the ice was loaded. It was shipped to the southern United States and around the world.

WEYMOUTH POND ICE. In March 1871, Alvin Hollis poses in South Weymouth with his ice wagon. Customers were promised "daily delivery" and "careful attention." Adapting to the seasons, Hollis also sold hay, grain, firewood, and flour. Demand for ice declined in the 1920s and 1930s, but the business survived by being flexible, adding coal, then oil, and most recently air-conditioning and plumbing services. The business is still family owned.

123

CATE'S WRAPPER FACTORY. Frederick Cate owned this factory at 23 Richmond Street, which made ladies' suits and wrappers (which were like aprons or house dresses). The house on the right is 21 Richmond Street.

THE IRONWORKS. Employees of the Weymouth Iron Company take a photograph break in front of the upper mill and the company's stone office building in the 1880s. The upper mill housed furnaces and the rolling machines that pressed the hot iron into plate form, from which nails were cut. The company also made side wheels and anchors. The ironworks can also be seen on page 76.

A MEAT WAGON. Howard Locke, who lived at 56 Park Avenue, sold only the best meat from his horse and wagon. After Locke died in 1908, his son Ray (pictured here) took over the business; in 1914, he sold steak for 29¢ per pound and fancy brisket for 21¢ per pound.

DOOR-TO-DOOR SALES. Because most housewives did not drive, vendors brought their products to the homes. Frank McPhee lived at 11 Torrey Street and sold nuts door-to-door c. 1915.

EDISON. The Charles Leavitt Edgar Station of the Edison Electric Illuminating Company of Boston was built on the Fore River in 1925, generating 72,000 kilowatts of energy. It housed the first high-pressure reheat unit ever installed in the United States but was removed in 1999 to make way for a new power plant.

WEYMOUTH HOSPITAL. The Reed estate, a three-story brick house and stable, was opened as Weymouth Hospital on May 21, 1922. The third floor had quarters for employees. Within six months, 207 patients had been admitted, exceeding the capacity of the hospital. As a result, a new wing was added and the stable was rebuilt as a nurses' home.

LOVELL'S GROVE. Once a thriving resort and amusement park that rivaled even Nantasket Beach, Lovell's Grove sat by Route 3A and drew tourists who arrived on the steamer passenger boat *Stamford*, which wove its way among the Harbor Islands as it traveled from Boston. After the gradual decline of the resort's popularity, the area was built up; much of the site was later occupied by the Edison Company coal wharf and power plant, which were constructed during the 1920s. The ship's terminal and the entrance, shown here, stood just to the east of where the Fore River Bridge stands today.

ACKNOWLEDGMENTS

This book would not have been possible without the support of dozens of Weymouth town employees, residents, and former residents. On behalf of the Weymouth Historical Society, we thank them all for their generosity.

In particular, Elizabeth (Sheppard) Murphy, the reference program supervisor at Tufts Library in Weymouth, provided invaluable assistance not only in locating photographs but also in tracking down details so that our captions would be accurate, entertaining, and informative. If she could not find the information we needed, she would find the telephone numbers of the people who would know. We simply could not have written the book without her; surely, she must be the best resource librarian the town has ever had.

Jennie Belcher and the late Harry Belcher donated pictures, scrapbooks of clippings, and personal files to the Weymouth Historical Society. These resources provided many of the dates, names, and other vital tidbits about the subjects of the older photographs. Donald Cormack came up with information and stories about most of the families in town, from 1900 to the present, at the drop of a hat. Donald and Bill Mathewson provided pictures and information on North Weymouth. Donald Sargent and Thomas Countie provided the pictures and information on the South Weymouth Naval Air Station.

Capt. Leo DeAngelo of the Weymouth Police Department donated most of the police department pictures. Lt. William Cope and Capt. James Thomas provided photographs and advice. Richard Pattison gave the history of the Weymouth Fire Department, along with pictures. Carol Kelly of the Weymouth Park Department provided photographs and information about the department.

We owe special thanks to the family and friends who ran errands, dug for pictures, made photocopies, helped with writing the captions, typed, and did all sorts of chores: Bob Johnson, Fran Merten, Jim and Joanne Palmieri, Bill Sargent, Marcia Sargent, Phil Smith, Megan Sullivan, Ryan Sullivan, and Liz Tighe.

Photographs, information, and advice were also provided by Leonard Bicknell, Gladys Blanchard, Mary Cole Brennan, Linda Chapman, Stu Chipman, Nancy Clark, Susan Clark, Velma Collyer, Bill Cope, Joe Costa, Elaine DeCosta, Marion DelVecchio, Chris and Larry DiBona, Jim Donaher, Carol and Bill Donovan, Jim Dwyer, Josie Fletcher, John Fraher, Ed Hines, Bob Hunt, Barbara and Bill Johnson, Sgt. Robert Johnson, Don Keene, Esther Kibby, Dave MacDonald, Joseph Merten, William Neiland, John F. Nolan Jr., Dick Ortenzi, Dick Pattison, Albert and Marilyn Perette, John Perette, Helena Reidy, Ernie Remondini, Anthony Sammarco, Helen Sargent, Francis Sheppard, Michael Stokes, Joseph Striano, Bill Tormey, and Ed Walker.

If we have forgotten to mention any of the people who helped us, please accept our apologies and consider our oversight to be the only negative side of the overwhelmingly generous responses we received to our requests for assistance.

128

www.ingramcontent.com/pod-product-compliance
Lightning Source LLC
Chambersburg PA
CBHW050611110426
42813CB00008B/2525